'Wit and wisdom do not always go together in this foolish world – but with Simon May they do, and we can all enjoy the result.'

Douglas Hurd, former British Foreign Secretary and former Chairman of the Booker Prize judges

'Distilled wisdom is rare and valuable; it is here in abundance.'

Peter Sutherland, Chairman, Goldman Sachs International and BP

'Fascinating and important insights of great practical value.'

Edward Heath, former British Prime Minister

THE LITTLE BOOK OF BIG THOUGHTS

To find my home in one sentence, concise, as if hammered in metal. Not to enchant anybody. Not to earn a lasting name in posterity. An unnamed need for order, for rhythm, for form, which three words are opposed to chaos and nothingness.

Czesław Miłosz, Poet and Nobel Laureate for Literature, *Unattainable Earth* (The Ecco Press, New York, 1986)

This delivering of knowledge in distinct and disjointed aphorisms doth leave the wit of man more free to turn and toss, and to make use of that which is so delivered to more several purposes and applications.

Francis Bacon, Philosopher, *Novum Organum* (1620)

THE LITTLE BOOK OF BIG THOUGHTS

SIMON MAY

metro

Published by Metro Publishing Ltd,
3, Bramber Court, 2 Bramber Road,
London W14 9PB, England

www.blake.co.uk

First published in paperback in 2005

ISBN 1 84358 150 7

British Library Cataloguing-in-Publication Data:

A catalogue record for this book is available from the British Library.

Design by www.envydesign.co.uk

Printed in Great Britain by Bookmarque

1 3 5 7 9 10 8 6 4 2

Papers used by Metro Publishing are natural, recyclable products
made from wood grown in sustainable forests. The manufacturing
processes conform to the environmental regulations of the country
of origin.

Every attempt has been made to contact the relevant copyright-
holders, but some were unobtainable. We would be grateful if
the appropriate people could contact us.

Cover photograph © Ian O'Leary Photography Ltd.

Contents

To my mother and to the memory
of my father.

INTRODUCTION

❧

EVERYONE CAN THINK. Thinking is not the preserve of writers or high-flyers or academic philosophers. In fact, some of the world's greatest sages, such as Jesus, Socrates, and the Buddha, were none of these things: they left no writings, they had no worldly positions, and they certainly had no philosophy degrees. Thinking constantly happens deep within each of us, usually unconsciously, stimulated by our experiences, our relationships, our work, our learning.

This collection of aphorisms is meant to aid readers in discovering their own ideas, in crystallizing their own thoughts – on truth, love, ambition, piety, ageing, haste, sincerity, cruelty, friendship, and other topics that we all eventually confront and that all ultimately point to one question: what is the best life for me to lead? Its aim is to provoke rather than instruct, to open paths to reflection rather than bring them to conclusions. Its method is to advance nuggets of thought which the reader can either accept or reject, embellish or complete, as he or she sees fit.

But what exactly are aphorisms? They are, quite simply, condensed ideas – sometimes descriptive (suggesting how things are), sometimes prescriptive (suggesting how things should be), sometimes merely taking the form of questions which hint at, but do not give, answers. Their subject can be broadly philosophical, scientific, or literary – with, from the mid-seventeenth century, a particular focus on human behaviour and its motivations. Their mood is either playful and humorous (if sometimes sardonic) or, more often in the history of aphorisms, serious and sententious (if sometimes satiric). Their length is anything from a couple of words to a paragraph – or, more rarely, a page – and their style is, correspondingly, pithy or discursive. Their language varies from the coolly clear, urbane, and categorical (as with La Rochefoucauld) to the more lyrical, oracular, and experimental (as with Nietzsche) – though, in all cases, the choice, order, and rhythm of words is crucial, and, in some cases, elaborate use is made of punning, ambiguity, and other verbal play. They are usually isolated, fragmentary statements – though any particular author's aphorisms, taken together, are likely to possess an underlying thematic and temperamental unity, and therefore to be systematic in spirit though not in scope or organization.

The uses of aphorisms, since their origin in ancient Greece, have been many and varied: in education, in criticism, in polemic, in moral or scientific inquiry, in reviving ancient wisdom, or simply in exploring new ideas or probing old ones. In some of these cases, they are also called 'maxims' – especially where their style is assertive rather than speculative and their purpose is to help establish, analyse, and assimilate rules for sound practical conduct, such as the medical maxims of Hippocrates (the 'father of medicine'), or the worldly maxims of Gracian (the seventeenth-century Spanish Jesuit), or the ethical maxims of Renaissance humanists like Erasmus and Thomas More. When they are sayings in much wider use, but expressed in some striking or novel manner, they are sometimes called 'adages' or 'proverbs'. They then express common or orthodox thoughts in uncommon or attention-grabbing styles, so that these thoughts can be readily noticed and digested by a wide, popular audience. Or they can be called 'epigrams', 'precepts', 'apophthegms', and the like – which are more or less the same thing.

More important than these definitions, however, is why we should bother at all with aphorisms – especially since they can be so frustratingly elusive, allusive, and inconclusive. The first reason, I suggest, is that it is these very qualities that truth itself seems to possess – or, rather, that our attempts to formulate truths possess, whether they are expressed in single sentences or are teased out into whole books. All these attempts seem necessarily provisional, incomplete, partisan – and aphorisms, with their isolated stabs at truth, can excellently reflect this partial experience of the world that appears to be our lot. Indeed, the capacity of the aphoristic form to express the fragmented and the indeterminate well suits it to an age like ours that, with the possible exception of certain natural sciences, has decisively turned its back on anything that strives to be total, systematic, and ultimate. Moreover, the fact that 'truth' is, in and of itself, a terminally enigmatic concept is indicated by the failure even of the greatest philosophers to define it satisfactorily, despite centuries of effort.

The second advantage of aphorisms is that a short, suggestive statement can hint at much more than it literally says – an allusiveness which continuous prose can have a harder job achieving. The combination of an abrupt, declarative style with a high degree of generalization and incompleteness – of precision with imprecision, or closedness with openness – is one way in which the good aphorism achieves this effect. Another is the deliberate use of paradox and ambiguity. Such devices exploit the fact that an aphorism, however polished, is inherently unfinished, and, however complex, brief enough for every word to command attention.

These two features of aphorisms – that they reflect the inevitable incompleteness of our claims to truth and that they can point to more than they say – were surely in the mind of Karl Kraus, the great Viennese satirist of the early twentieth century, when he claimed that 'an aphorism never coincides with the truth: it is either a half-truth or one-and-a-half truths.' And these two features enable aphorisms to address a related dilemma: we need concepts and languages to say anything true at all, yet those very concepts and languages seem to be insurmountable barriers to truth. This is akin to the old conundrum that words can get us only so far, that the deepest truths may be better discerned non-verbally, such as in music and dance, or even in silence. Because of its brevity, the aphorism not only recognizes the necessary modesty of words by quite explicitly using the minimum number possible; it can also make a virtue of this necessity by playing on imprecision – and on all that is, and must be allowed to remain, shadowy, indefinable, and intangible. In a sense, therefore, the aphorism is suspended between language and silence – between striving to say it all and striving to say nothing.

Thirdly, aphorisms can be a more enjoyable stimulus to reflection than longer texts – because of their variety, because they invite diverse interpretations, and because their compactness makes them such clear targets – for agreement or disagreement. In addition, by jumping from one subject to another, they are better at catching our minds off guard and so at ambushing our preconceptions – an effect which is particularly well achieved by authors, such as Lichtenberg, who present their aphorisms in no particular thematic order. Though random ordering is in many ways more entertaining than the formality of subject-headings, I have opted for the latter both for ease of reference and to preserve the links, overt and covert, between different thoughts on the same theme.

Some of these aphorisms are best mulled over alone. Others are most enjoyably read with a companion. Socrates insisted that we best uncover – and clarify – our innermost thoughts in discussion, rather than in isolation. He conversed with anyone who was curious: craftsmen, traders, politicians, harlots, the young and the old. His venue – the origin, in many respects, of Western philosophy – was the market-place, not the university lecture hall; his method dialogue, not monologue. For he understood what our time is rediscovering:

that communication is the royal route to knowing ourselves and to approaching truth, that the 'Me' and the 'We' are, in a crucial sense, not competitive but complementary.

Though aphorisms are ideal for an age like ours that mistrusts systems and worships the fragmentary, they are, as I have already indicated, not a modern invention. They go back to such great figures in antiquity as Heraclitus, Hippocrates, Theognis, and Seneca. They reappeared in the Renaissance, like so many other classical idioms, when they were cultivated as a distinct literary form by Erasmus, Paracelsus, Montaigne, and a succession of French philosophers. They flowered in the seventeenth century with thinkers like Pascal and La Rochefoucauld in France, Gracian in Spain, and Bacon in England. From the mid-eighteenth to the mid-twentieth centuries, the masters of the aphoristic form include Lichtenberg, Schopenhauer, and Nietzsche in Germany, Wittgenstein and Kraus in Austria, Kafka in Prague, Emerson and Bradley in the United States, and Kierkegaard in Denmark. In addition, some wonderful aphorisms can be culled from sources as diverse as Shakespeare and Woody Allen, Goethe and Monty Python, Oscar Wilde and the Marx brothers. A few of my own aphorisms deliberately respond to, contradict, or embellish those of certain earlier writers, notably Kafka, Kierkegaard, and Nietzsche.

This genre has been neglected since the end of the Second World War. However, with the death of ideology and the attraction of our age (for good or ill) to finding intimacy with vital aspects of life rather than to seizing the whole world with one commanding vision, now may be the right time to return to the aphoristic form, and so to recognize the deeply unsystematic nature of most living and thinking.

1

RELATING

The better one knows someone, the harder it is to recognize them.

❖

It is less awkward to be humane than to be human.

❖

People who cannot stand solitude find it hard to be intimate.

❖

How marvellous to be seen; how perilous to be dreamed of.

The highest joy of friendship – higher even than the delight of shared ideals – is to witness and defend another's life.

❖

Sometimes one can liberate others only if one is enslaved oneself.

❖

Tact is the most agreeable form of intimidation.

❖

Only the unreasonable expect others to be logical.

❖

Undesired praise can be as intrusive as unjust criticism.

❖

We often admire (or despise) people in order not to get to know them.

❧

To feel equal to others is almost always harder than to feel inferior or superior.

❧

Some enjoy others' suffering merely to enjoy their own safety.

❧

People(s) who are kindest to outsiders are often unkindest to each other.

❧

It can take more fortitude to sustain the tender emotions than the vehement ones.

❧

Vagueness can destroy human relations as thoroughly as can aggression.

Jealousy imprisons – but is it not also a craving of the imprisoned?

❧

We are usually too slow to trust those we love and too quick to trust those we need.

❧

Almost everything can be tolerated – as long as we do not know what we want.

❧

Unshakeable patience with others can awaken them more powerfully than the best instruction.

❧

Judge a person less by his actions than by what they collectively make of him.

❧

The deep can be faster to fathom than the superficial.

To seek 'total love' is as illusive – and destructive – as to seek total knowledge.

❧

Greed often finds more pleasure in taking from others than in giving to itself.

❧

Guilt keeps one loyal to one's own values, shame to the values of people one needs.

❧

The only 'natural enemies' are those who take one's very nature as an offence.

❧

Little is so strenuous as *keeping* someone soothed.

❧

Generous pity: to heed, embolden, defend another. Selfish pity: to hide, hijack, flee into their distress.

❖

It is less suffering itself that evokes unbearable pity than *surrender* before suffering.

❖

Loneliness can be fiercest in the company of others.

❖

Insincere compliments should always be returned.

❖

Deep disputes get solved only after exhausting their relevance or their participants.

❖

We seldom convince anyone of what they do not already believe.

❧

Sometimes we trust only because prudence seems too arduous.

❧

Gifts from the generous unite; gifts from the mean divide. (The miser resents you for making his gift *necessary*.)

❧

Power over others can be the subtlest form of slavery.

❧

It is easy to be lawful, difficult to be just.

❧

Resilient institutions, like resilient marriages, transform goodwill from an occasional blessing into a permanent duty.

❧

Some admire their intimates only in order to admire their choices.

❧

Hear others' silence; heed their solitude. Otherwise they cannot be known.

❧

The terrible danger in the present age is to treat everything – and everyone – *experimentally*.

❧

A great friendship is always more exalted than either of its participants.

❧

Much can be tolerated only by forgiving it.

2

TIMING

Nothing is deeply experienced – or revealed – unless one encounters it at the right pace. (Music, love, nature, knowledge...)

❖

The ambitious person has no time to hurry.

❖

An idea that appears to us 'in a flash' has usually matured secretly for years.

❖

There is no greater danger to one's maturation than the headlong rush to define who one is.

❖

Reason's great enemy is not the cult of irrationalism – which still venerates the authentic – but the culture of speed.

❖

Life cannot be lived to the full by attempting to live every moment to the limit.

❖

All haste wears a death mask.

3

GRATITUDE

Sometimes only gratitude can bind us to what eludes our grasp – our past, our beloved, our world, our fate.

❧

Thanking, like thinking, must deeply engage with its objects if it is not politely to detach one from them.

❧

If we are to live life fully, we must not be *too* grateful to it – else we stifle the innocence and rebellion which, in due measure, a vigorous life demands.

❧

Gratitude can be our ultimate openness to the world; or it can be our last defence against misfortune – and perhaps the strongest.

4

PRIDE

The oldest consolation for failure: 'He is successful; but I am purer, higher.'

❧

Many accuse themselves in order to believe that they are better than they are.

❧

It is tempting to consider what is beyond our power to be beneath our dignity.

❧

For the hermetic pride, all intimacy is a trap.

❧

Narcissism, like vanity, springs from self-*mistrust*.

❧

We tend to love our conviction more than our convictions.

❧

The charm of repentance is to ease the pain of errors – not to prevent their recurrence.

❧

The proud rely on their own self-esteem; the vain solicit it from others.

❧

Many who cannot save themselves long to save the world.

❧

Humility is commonly employed not only for making light of failure but for refusing to be encumbered by success.

-ᕙ-

Pride spins more lies than do even envy or ambition.

-ᕙ-

Vanity is a hydra with many heads, lust a monster with only one – and by far the more tractable for that.

-ᕙ-

5

LOVING...

We are all too often attracted to what is different in another, but nourish in them only what is similar to ourselves.

❧

The shortest distance between two hearts is seldom a straight line.

❧

Love, in its extreme attentiveness, accumulates a great trail of doubts – and then, from its deep power of acceptance, *jettisons* them.

❧

To favour oneself over one's neighbour is easy;
to love oneself over him can be a good deal
harder.

❧

Intense self-content and -contempt can both
occasion a great urge to love others – in order to
flee the enigma of oneself.

❧

Lovers idealize not only the beloved, but
themselves as well; for through love they
visualize, however dimly, *their own*
perfectibility.

❧

Open-ended receptivity to someone's reality
can be more intimate than the most passionate
devotion.

❧

The deeper a disagreement, the harder for both sides to agree what it is really about.

❦

It is a great mystery that another person can find in you a lifelong source of reassurance that you cannot for a moment detect in yourself.

❦

It can be easier, because more passive, to love those who hurt us than those who fortify us.

❦

To many who are hungry for love, poison tastes sweetest of all.

❦

Those who consider their love sacrificial invariably want it repaid in hard cash.

❦

To be the perfect spouse would ruin any
marriage.

❖

In love, some attack so as to surrender, others
surrender so as to attack.

❖

To invite love is hard; to repel it is almost
impossible.

❖

It is easy to be liked by people whom we do not
love.

❖

Anyone who resents the intrusion and
possessiveness of love resents the love itself.

❖

The mistrustful resist love for years; and then, exhausted by isolation, suddenly trust with arbitrary abandon.

❧

Dread lies near the beginning of love – of man as of God.

❧

Solitude is best when it can be shared with a loved one.

❧

Love makes much possible, but little attainable.

❧

Love's wisest demand: that the other person return to himself.

❧

Love's darkness: to live the other's deadness.

.6

...AND HOW
TO STAY LOVED

No relationship would be sealed without
mutual incomprehension.

❧

People *continue* to like us mainly for the
weaknesses of our strengths.

❧

Tenderness, playfulness, and reverence form
the centre of gravity of all love – without which
it lacks balance and fails to mature.

❧

It is all too easy – and risky – for relationships
to be cemented by their sadnesses.

The faults of loved ones can be tolerated and even enjoyed – provided they have nothing in common with one's own.

❧

To remain in people's affection it is usually safest to be dead.

7

SUFFERING

Many fuss over others' suffering – even God's –
in order to forget their own.

❖

Some tolerate an inert life only by going insane
on purpose.

❖

We excuse our mistakes in six ways: by
diminishing them, by regretting them, by seeing
them as inevitable, by focusing on their causes,
by seeking the good in them, and by enjoying
our survival of them. Here even the nonchalant
are diligent!

❖

It can be dangerously tempting to love life in general in order to escape life in particular.

❖

The destitute lack the safety to feel self-pity.

❖

Sometimes we forgive out of love, but too often we forgive out of *fear* – in order to imagine mastering an offender whom we feel too weak to avenge.

❖

Ingratitude is how we tolerate the burden of others' kindness.

❖

All suffering strives to establish its value – and so to 'redeem' itself.

8

DECEIVING

It is hard to succeed in the world without the skill to claim credit where it is not due.

❧

Fraud and deception are most strictly forbidden to those who cannot conceal them.

❧

Clever thieves do not steal; they lay claim – artfully.

❧

The proliferation of 'rights' has greatly enriched the discipline of theft.

❧

Indignation enables us to lie with a good conscience – and, when merited, loses much of its charm.

❧

The eyes, far from being a window to the soul, can dissemble greatly; the mouth less so; the hands least of all.

❧

Sentimentality mimics passions which it wishes to enjoy but cannot experience.

❧

There are only two things which, given sufficient desire, close friends feel entirely justified in stealing: your books and your spouse.

❧

An act of weakness is most endearingly presented as a decision of principle.

Our large faults are best concealed by parading our small ones.

❧

People always seem most naked when they are flimsily concealed.

❧

Affectations can be delightful embellishments – to a natural personality.

❧

Sincerity is the easiest virtue to fake.

9

TALKING

People are more alike in speech than in silence.

❧

Chatter about 'creativity' paralyses creation.

❧

Silence is the most insidious form of revenge –
for *both* sides.

❧

Solemn crowds are beautiful; solemn
individuals are ugly.

❧

Excessive talk silences the individual in one.

❖

A real listener hears you even when you keep quiet.

10

KNOWING

What cannot be taught always needs the greatest learning.

❖

To know much is easy; to digest much is hard.

❖

Only a light spirit can bear heavy knowledge. (More generally: how the light supports the heavy.)

❖

It can be easiest to tell the truth when one is not being sincere.

❖

To the extent that thought is an ordered
relationship between *experienced* passions,
thinking and feeling are one.

❧

To find oneself stretched between opposed
convictions can be the spark of life; and, in a
well-formed character, the sharper their
contradictions the brighter the light.

❧

To succeed, one must question the value of
one's works, but never the value of one's work.

❧

We can deeply love what we do not know, but
we cannot deeply know what we do not love.

❧

We find the universal only after prolonged
encounter with the particular – and only if we
do not grope after it too insistently.

Every adequate explanation ends up turning the familiar into the mysterious.

❧

Irony is a marvellous spice of life, but a paralysing way of life.

❧

The homeless best divine the minds of others – including God.

❧

Experience no more makes us wise than hearing notes makes us musical; for both demand the prior capacity to discern *innate structure*.

❧

One *really* knows only what one's nature and experience prepare one to know. All other knowledge is for distraction or titillation or prestige, and is consequently never properly understood.

The urge to create – deeds, books, monuments, power – is inextricably bound up with the need to forget: that is, to so order the world that it will have no room for what we wish not to remember.

❧

The spirit – even more than the body – develops strength and subtlety only in small, indistinguishable steps. All great 'leaps' just manifest an accumulation of such steps – or else are not genuine.

❧

Joy and pain not only go together, they grow together: for the commitments in which we find meaning usually bring us sadness too.

❧

It can take a lot of dung to produce an exquisite flower.

The three transfiguring passions: love, despair, and disgust.

❧

Doubt can attack one dogma only in the name of another.

❧

A mind that moves too swiftly cannot pause to think.

❧

Learning should always enrich one's ignorance.

❧

All maturation involves hard-won losses.

❧

Only a rich imagination can deeply fathom reality.

❧

One can grasp the world too powerfully to create it.

❧

Most acute presence of mind is also bodily.

11

INDULGENCE AND RETICENCE

The best seducers are themselves the hardest to seduce.

❖

The great ascetic abstains not from sensuality but from love: indeed, only through sensuality can he tolerate this much larger denial.

❖

A reserve of crudity remains in even the most highly cultivated people, and without it the raw power on which great refinement constantly draws would simply ebb away.

❖

Everything beautiful feels at once intensely intimate, unreachably remote, and deeply necessary – and that is how it casts its spell.

❧

Every life of extreme dedication is experienced as essentially artificial; yet only under this unnatural pressure can a person's real nature flourish.

❧

In all except the prodigiously gifted, intense experience demands sporadic asceticism: for the world *floods* in only if it is intermittently dammed out.

❧

Reason leads us away from our emotions – and then deeper back into them.

❧

To relish the extremes of discipline and dissipation, stability and chaos, implies no contradiction: for intense opposites relieve not merely each other but also one's inner deadness and disorientation.

❧

All fervency – whether for one's loves, one's hatreds, one's work, one's country – has the quality of prayer.

❧

Force seldom instils, or defeats, a belief – without the help of isolation.

❧

The morbidity of individuals is as unique as their smell.

❧

Every mood, including sadness, has its own coquetry.

❧

Passions mature best in a fastidious heart.

❧

Most people would be ashamed if they had never sinned.

12

ESCAPING

We all too often seek new opportunities so as not to seize existing ones.

❦

To take refuge in something – art, virtue, friendship, nature, God – unfailingly delights us, but is never the best way of knowing or honouring it.

❦

Modesty shields us from others, humility from ourselves.

❦

It usually takes several generations before a family can laugh at itself.

When life gets too tedious, disgust quickly
re-enchants it.

❧

The whole point of a good intention can be to
avoid a good action.

❧

Many fight for their principles; few live for them.

❧

Truth often hides itself by stepping forward as
a formula.

❧

An eye (or age) too eager for paradox can blind
itself to genuine contradiction.

❧

The great peril of feeling powerless is to seek a
life immune to powerlessness – and so to the
world itself.

Few *émigrés* can halt the act of escaping – which only becomes more subtle, more arbitrary, more inward.

❖

The ability to forget and the inability to recall are altogether different skills.

❖

To live in perpetual hope can be a form of resignation.

❖

Absorbing, but not passionate, activity is the most durable of all sedatives.

❖

We can become so sensitive to pain that we no longer notice it through a haze of minor irritations.

❖

It can be all too tempting to abandon the risks of love for the pleasures of sympathy.

❖

The pathos of regret can blind us to our real mistakes.

❖

The only advantage of habitual pessimism is to protect one from genuine despair.

❖

Earnestness of mood is a sly way of escaping seriousness of purpose.

❖

To hide inconspicuously, choose the company of aliens.

❖

Sometimes privacy can be secured only by forcing others to despise one.

❖

One can become a parent without training – but not a butcher.

❖

Most criticize the world not in order to change it but in order to flee it.

❖

The stubborn are the hardest to pin down.

❖

How principled and passionate indecisiveness can be!

The true cynic expects nothing more from life than confirmation of his disappointments.

❖

When disillusionment needs relief, it often turns romantic.

❖

The most powerful fantasies are those with the firmest roots in reality.

13

THE DIVINE

It is indecent to invoke God merely to explain the incomprehensible.

❖

Among those harmed by idolatry we seldom count the idols themselves.

❖

Virtually any value, ideal, or god can be employed for evil as well as for good; that it has been so employed is never, therefore, an adequate reason for abandoning it.

❖

Modern scepticism has left our religious hunger to scavenge for scraps of superstition.

To save gods from being desecrated by men
and men from never regaining trust in gods, it is
in the interests of both men and gods finally to
keep a respectful distance from one another.

❖

The transcendent – a great presence that
language cannot express and we cannot possess
– may hide or be unheard, but will never 'die'.

❖

Culture, unlike civilization, is innately pious –
and so are all its rebels and ironists.

❖

How unbearably lonely is the god who is only
either worshipped or denied – and who cannot
end this isolation even by becoming man.

❖

Science and religion fight – and unite – as only
brothers can.

All attempts to justify the possibility of evil –
as, say, necessary to freedom or to attaining the
good – are not only unintelligible but
sacrilegious; for they presume to explain the
ways of God from the perspective of a god.

❧

God – the timeless, monotheistic God –
temporarily abolished ancestor-worship; but with
his untimely 'death' we *are* our past again, and
without due deference to it we commit suicide.

❧

Only the pure are purified by religion.

❧

Who wants a god that is satisfied with
humanity?

14

FINDING OUR WAY

The most seductive goals are those that enable us to find a path but to lose our way.

❧

New intentions and 'fresh starts' are life's hardest narcotics.

❧

Well-being, unlike passing pleasures, cannot be directly grasped; but a life of sustained devotion to things we love can sporadically bestow it upon us.

❧

To understand what we are, we may first need to understand what we are not – and, sometimes, this means temporarily entertaining, and even *becoming*, precisely what is most dangerously alien to ourselves.

❧

Occasionally we can seek – and find – freedom only by building prisons for ourselves.

❧

One's deepest values – those that years of doubt and opposition fail to undermine but, on the contrary, strengthen – can only be discovered, never created.

❧

All joy – even in hitherto unknown territories – is a sort of homecoming.

❧

We cannot find ourselves unless we find good in the world.

❧

Few paths to health do not take a detour through sickness.

❧

We sterilize life by reviewing it before it has occurred.

❧

Better to have great love for little things than little love for great things.

❧

To be strong you must trust yourself; to be merely resilient you need not.

❧

Suffering may be life's great teacher, but few learn more from it than sufferance.

Promises to oneself should be as binding as promises to others.

❧

Nothing really functions as a means unless we engage in it as an end.

❧

We necessarily believe more than we can know.

❧

To thrive one must be patient enough to build one's skills from the bottom up and incautious enough to throw oneself open to the four winds of chance.

❧

Seek yourself too directly – and you will discover nothing.

❧

'Conscience' is that alertness to guiding values
– and to the need for guiding values – without
which our finest powers are incapacitated.

❖

One can command oneself only if one can
dedicate oneself.

❖

True cunning is getting one's way without
having to ask for it.

❖

Without deadly opponents it is hard to find
the *real* courage of one's convictions.

❖

We can believe in so much and yet take a stand
on so little.

❖

Some freedoms can be conferred; most are attained by fighting the countless seductions of slavery.

❧

Most virtues, untamed, can become as tyrannical as any vice – but, because they do so on behalf of what we consider good, it is much harder to detect their trail of destruction.

❧

On the whole, we repudiate vices not because we find them wicked but because we find them vulgar.

❧

To create a persona mix four parts fakery with one part sincerity and stir well..

❧

Few discover themselves without pretence.

❧

We see because we have found a path; we do not find a path because we can see.

❖

The authentic is where home and exile meet.

❖

The superstitious usually get unlucky.

❖

So tenaciously do we cling to our inherited values that we can embrace new ones only in the name of the old – and any revolution in values or repudiation of one's age is, therefore, always incomplete.

15

SURVIVING

Many things are most lovable when we have
conquered bitter disappointment in them.

❖

One does not get 'beyond' anything unless one
has been immersed in it.

❖

Few of our deep problems can be resolved;
most must be outgrown.

❖

Suffering indeed strengthens – the strong.

❖

Most explanations bore us – except as
consolations.

We learn the real lessons of our blunders best when we are poised to repeat them.

❧

Misfortune cannot be mastered simply by practising detachment or justifying its value; one must first absorb its cold necessity.

❧

One must know what to look for if one is to know what to overlook.

❧

Most of the wounds inflicted by truth can be healed only by more truth.

❧

The fastest antidote to a fear is *another* fear.

❧

We always inherit the sins of our forefathers; but occasionally we are also able to repudiate them.

❖

The innocently punished fervently seek their crimes; the justly punished tend to be rather less diligent.

❖

There are four possible reactions to the horrors of the world – and so to the world itself: to justify, to ignore, to accept, or to repudiate. (Of which the most nonsensical, but still popular, is the first.)

❖

Frivolity is most resolute in those whom love has first exhausted and then eluded.

Our feelings must remain vibrant, fresh, light –
even when they are sad, even when they age.

❧

The past – like unrequited love – is always
buried alive.

❧

Apology as anaesthesia.

❧

Some mistakes are too good to be regretted.

❧

Even more destructive than bad luck is our
resentment of it.

❧

Few of our trials actually happen.

16

AGEING

It can take half a lifetime for one's different personalities to *trust* each other.

❖

It is an endlessly subtle and gradual task to let go of infantility.

❖

Faces that age without maturing grow formless: dead before they die.

❖

People quietly disdain anyone they are confident of outliving, whatever his merits; for in this sole respect, at least, they are the victor and he the already vanquished.

Wisdom and generosity often bloom in youth; but nuance and magnanimity ripen only with time.

❧

A turning-point in life is the realization that the opportunity for 'fresh starts' is over. One then either harnesses oneself brutally, or fumbles forever.

❧

It is sterile to contemplate the nature of Death, but empowering to think towards one's *own* death.

❧

The art of dying well should be at least on a par with the science of obstetrics.

❧

Youth has strength without patience, age patience without strength; but our best years have both.

❖

To see pure goodness in little children is an immaculate deception.

❖

The craving for health easily becomes a sickness.

17

SLANDERING

The laziest way to respect oneself is to resent others.

❖

We often condemn what we lack the nerve to confront – including ourselves.

❖

The lure of slander is the lure of all extremes: to believe something with promiscuous clarity.

❖

A personality is most simply constructed on a scaffolding of hate.

❖

The urge to define oneself through revulsion for others – individuals, classes, races, nations – and the drawing of *genuine* strength from this enmity, is perhaps the most terrible fact of human nature.

❖

Hatred, like love, has a taste for its own sacredness – and thence for the sacred itself.

❖

Racism's overwhelming subtlety, scale, and resilience are systematically underrated – especially by its victims.

❖

Hostility to something easily blinds one to its real faults.

❖

Malicious gossip is most distressing when it is true.

Some cling to their scapegoats for dear life.

Few forgive those whom they have wronged.

Mischievous tales need the best wags.

18

EVIL

Evil's six most subversive habits: to turn virtue over to the service of vice; to invert values in such a way as to make what is dead seem alive and what is alive seem dead; to shame another into repudiating what he naturally loves; to invoke the sacred to justify the corrupt; to incite jealousy, fear, or hatred between people; to parade power-lust as *love*.

❧

Our greatest illusion about evil is that it knows it is evil; whereas, in fact, the most dreadful destroyers, and the ones most indifferent to forgiveness, are precisely those who 'know not what they do'.

❧

Though blood-lust can be aroused in almost anyone, more violence is fuelled by yearning for comfort than by joy in cruelty.

❧

Evil may be outwardly 'banal'; but inwardly it always rages – with confusion, despair, anger, pride.

❧

Brutality often invigorates itself by turning sentimental.

❧

Can extreme sensitivity to pain be a cause of savagery – especially in its more sophisticated forms – as well as a result? (The twentieth century.)

❧

Our cruelty has many means, including kindness.

❖

Hell is far more restrained than inhumanity: at least it grants its victims trial by an omniscient and impartial judge.

19

OPENING-UP TO LIFE...

The distinction: to possess versus to love –
closure to the essence of things or openness to
it. (And yet, *the* identity: for the one cannot
exist without the other.)

❧

Many things refuse us intimacy unless we can
already say farewell to them – and foremost
among these is life itself.

❧

To be fully contemporary one cannot be a
child only of one's time; one should also seek
adoption by at least one other century.

❧

Destiny, like a lover, is one of those awkward things of which we must be simultaneously slave and master.

❧

One can expand one's horizons only by imposing borders on one's spirit.

❧

Tentatively to praise what we find alien or distasteful can be the only way of approaching it closely, and so of properly determining our attitude to it.

❧

Instead of worrying about the future we should strive for precise attunement to the present – and only then might we divine what is to come.

❧

One gets to know the world best neither by immersing oneself in the fray nor by withdrawal into slowness, but by alternating between the two.

❧

All freedom is bought at the price of accepting constraint, dependence, and inevitability – the constraint of self-discipline, the dependence of love, and the inevitability of the world as it is.

❧

Relations between trust and fear are always immoderate: a little trust can banish a huge amount of fear, while a breath of mistrust can reap a whirlwind of fear.

❧

No one can inspire greater fortitude than the dead whom one loves – not even one's deadliest enemy.

Our experiences must always master us before we can successfully master them.

❧

Hypocrisy is often the first step towards an open mind.

❧

Failure is life's magnifying glass.

❧

Solitude is good; isolation is bad.

❧

Humility as total listening; faith as total hearing.

❧

Why are 'live' and 'love' separated only by a vowel?

❧

To possess wholly we must submit wholly.

❧

Affirming engages; justifying estranges.

❧

Opportunities are best created by seizing them.

20

...AND CLOSING-UP

We often evaluate things in order not to experience them.

❖

Gloom – like hope – can be our cosiest bolt-hole.

❖

To want something too urgently is always to lose its essence.

❖

To deem all existence vain is itself a judgement of the utmost vanity.

❖

Meanness asphyxiates; generosity frees –
oneself before all others.

❧

The famous usually become deaf to everything
except applause.

❧

Sloth can be a full-time job – for those in a
state of siege against life.

❧

Pragmatism is seldom a guarantee of realism.

❧

We often chase the 'why' in order to blind
ourselves to the 'what'.

❧

Truth is cruellest when it kills our love for
something.

Life is too easily spent somewhere between the exhaustion of negating it and the terror of living it.

❖

Those who want to be wholly right never seem to be wholly real.

❖

The final indictment by this age of critics will be that there is nothing left worth criticizing.

❖

Technology's most pervasive danger is not its power to destroy but its ingenuity to distract.

❖

Action is seldom as reasonable as inertia.

❖

Our age is intensely animated yet curiously detached.

❧

Can anything, even a thought, be *possessed* for long without evicting its magic?

21

ATTAINING·STUPIDITY

Superlatives maim.

❧

Complaining stupefies.

❧

Indifference lames the heart.

❧

What we measure we diminish.

❧

Stupidity needs stubbornness to make it truly stupid.

❧

The inveterate spectator of life imagines that, by chaining himself to the world with judgements, he will finally become one with it.

❖

There is no surer route to a petty mind than an obsession with refuting the pettiness of others.

❖

Those who strain for great 'vision' usually see only mirages.

❖

Whatever detaches makes stupid: above all, arrogance, mistrust, and fear.

❖

Many seek freedom in violently discarding their talents and judgement – while conserving a secret ballast of sanity to save them from destruction.

Self-haters seldom see themselves clearly
enough to be self-critical.

❧

Stupidity is mentor to whole classes of
shrewdness.

❧

Our deepest beliefs are all too often our most
superficial.

❧

Some large ideas find space only in an empty
mind.

❧

Almost every 'nothing but' that reduces the
complex to the simple is mere hocus-pocus –
which makes vanish whatever it seeks to explain.

❧

Dogmatism is vulgar, even when it is insincere.

The wise are much more susceptible to fools
than fools are to the wise.

❧

The yearning for truth, being a form of love,
can foster terrible illusion.

❧

Most 'realism' impoverishes reality.

❧

Only greed will serve *any* god.

22

MEANING IN LIFE

We can happily bear meanings that avoid life, but never lives that avoid meaning.

❖

One's supreme values always seem absolute – even when one repudiates the absolute.

❖

To see meaning in one's life is to express exactly what one has become – and so is never a 'decision'.

❖

We value our choices more than we choose our values.

The 'fundamentalist' urge to rank the original above what developed out of it is no more reasonable than to deem the acorn superior to the oak.

❖

Great ideas are seldom refuted, just superseded.

❖

People – and ages – can practise abolishing a faith, just as they can practise believing in it.

❖

Our history, true or imagined, teaches us who we are – not how to act.

❖

It is rare to fathom what anything means to us except by experiencing its loss.

❖

Man *loves* the ethical only as his ultimate guarantor of order.

❧

The mere existence of something overwhelms all its other significances.

❧

One really knows the worth of a value only by pursuing its consequences to their limit.

❧

Most pessimists do not despise; they are indifferent: they damn not with low value but with no value.

❧

The 'digressions' of life often render an intensity of meaning that its overall trajectory refuses to yield.

❧

Few values can be destroyed by war. Fewer can ultimately survive thought.

❧

Three marks of all excellence, whether or not it is to our particular taste, are power, structure, and refinement.

❧

One seeks meaning in order to find happiness (despite its attendant sorrow); but one does not necessarily seek happiness in order to find meaning.

❧

Morality and religion are like husbands and wives: usually one serves the other; sometimes one undermines the other; and only rarely do they make an equal match.

❧

In a godless world, it all of a sudden takes courage to despise life.

❖

Modernity's self-torture: to repudiate itself in the name of *its own* supreme value – that of individual authenticity.

❖

Fanfares for 'cultural diversity' have come just when most of it has gone.

❖

The world is increasingly greedy for its liberation and increasingly numbed by its liberty.

❖

What marks out the West is not only its love of ideals, but its urge to abandon them.

❖

Only unattainable ideals can endure: for only they offer inexhaustible hope – and only they escape the banality of success.

❧

Would a civilization less fixated by time than ours be less respectful of truth?

❧

Obsession with the 'meaning' and 'value' of everything cripples our capacity for intimacy with anything.

❧

Death is the end of time that gives all time its weight.

❧

Only human nature does not abhor a vacuum.

❧

The value of existence can never be justified –
only affirmed.

❖

In the beginning was the word – but before that
came the deed.

❖

Where there is sun, there are usually shadows.

23

CHARACTER

The incorruptible can defiantly withstand great loss.

❖

Simplicity is the most complex attainment – because it demands the most perfect conquest of one's inner chaos.

❖

One's mind must be fathomed in solitude and one's character in community; but neither can be developed except by immersion in both.

❖

If we cannot outgrow our destructive passions we must outwit them – by forcibly and cunningly imagining their opposites.

❖

Bad taste is a harsher indictment than bad judgement – for taste manifests the whole individual, and so can be neither an 'error' nor, in its essentials, reformed.

❖

Self-knowledge always reflects a fine spirit but seldom creates one.

❖

Virtue without humanity can be as monstrous as humanity without virtue.

❖

The passion for justice has all the other passions ranged against it.

Suffering is fertile only when it both purifies *and* fortifies.

❖

Talent must be dwarfed by character – or it will not only fail, but attack its owner.

❖

Unless we constantly hone the skill of listening, the lies pile ever higher – and even the most sincere are unaware of them.

❖

Intellect is blind without emotion, and emotion is formless without intellect.

❖

Everyone is born into slavery; yet only the few seek freedom.

❖

A broad education civilizes less reliably than a narrow set of rules.

❖

Fear can be an amazing coward when it realizes that you intend to subdue it – and stunningly brazen at all other times.

❖

One easily forgets to cultivate the talents – of discipline, attention, and love – needed to cultivate all talents.

❖

Character and taste are cousins – and without them learning is arid, choice impotent, and emotion mere gesture.

❖

Only the generous can receive – wholeheartedly.

Passion, proportion, and judgement: the
girders of the soul.

❧

A 'free' will can trust itself – and especially its
safety.

❧

Character, like 'spirituality', is not
gregariousness; it is form.

24

CORRUPTION

Power corrupts; but powerlessness corrupts absolutely.

❧

Truth might not be absolute, but it can certainly be abused.

❧

To deify the human is to deaden it: everything in man is denatured by making it holy. (Art, love, virtue…)

❧

It is not ill-gotten gains themselves which presage disaster so much as the fatally liquid personality that pursues them.

The ferocity it takes to resist inhumanity easily makes people inhuman – even if their nature is gentle...*precisely* if it is gentle.

❧

How many miscreants who are 'only obeying rules' would *be* anybody without the rules and without the obeying?

❧

Envy fastens only on what it can imagine enjoying. The unreachable it merely admires.

❧

Always seek the noblest company – a hard rule when we crave companionship, for the ignoble have a sixth sense for that craving and are the first to fuel and feed it.

❧

Those who exaggerate everything lose conviction in anything – even themselves.

A life dominated by fear and hope dissolves the character, but leaves our cruder appetites perfectly intact.

❖

The cruel are seldom so unhappy: for they deaden their own sensitivity, love, and discernment, and thus the sources of most unhappiness.

❖

To isolate oneself from the world out of disgust at its corruption is dangerous; for isolation quickly makes one disorientated – and thus corrupt.

❖

The greatest danger of despair is to see the ethical as pointless.

❖

Captivity corrupts its captives – by forcing them to *love* it.

❧

A person's taste can never be eradicated, but can easily be incapacitated.

❧

Incessant judgers never dispense justice.

❧

The indifferent are the most uncritically critical.

❧

Not all impatience is a vice, but all vices may be forms of impatience.

25

SELF-ESTEEM

Self-esteem can be so arbitrary – and precarious – because it largely depends on which pieces in our great mosaic of virtues and vices we happen to be attending to.

❖

We can no more grasp our inner life than we can grasp our internal organs.

❖

A little reason vindicates one's beliefs; a lot unsettles them.

❖

One's life can only be lived forwards and described backwards, but whether it can be understood, let alone justified, in either direction is very doubtful.

❧

The real beauty of admitting to errors is to furnish proof of one's existence.

❧

Praise is best from our superiors – from those who relate more deeply to our attainments than we ourselves can.

❧

Ambitions rarely satisfy; they are usually overshadowed by others or exhausted by time.

❧

Fame makes snobs even of the wisest: for only by clinging to other celebrities are the famous reassured of the resilience, grandeur, and *fatedness* of their status.

❧

Peace of mind depends on the unprovable and is destroyed by the unlikely.

❧

Much sadness is merely weariness – whether from action or inaction.

❧

Only self-love can never be fully requited.

26

VALUES AND
THEIR VICES

Just as most virtues can be perverted into vices, so most vices contain the seeds of virtues.

❖

Values are cannibalistic. The idea that they tolerate 'pluralism' is ridiculous.

❖

One of the errors fostered by truthfulness is to stop believing in truth.

❖

Loyalty, pity, forgiveness, self-sacrifice: all can be most ardently reserved for those we dread but dare not hate, reject but dare not flee, fear but cannot master.

Certain flaws take superior talent, just as certain talents take superior flaws. (Love, courage, curiosity…: we possess their strengths only when captive to their weaknesses.)

❖

What is excellent is almost inevitably costly, but what is costly is not necessarily excellent.

❖

Irony, modernity's perfected art, playfully poisons the very culture whose 'absolutism' it set out to cure.

❖

To seek perfect autonomy is to treat everything – especially oneself – provisionally and thus unseriously.

❖

Novelty has become so automatic that it will soon need to be re-invented.

For the sake of originality, many prefer a desert where they can stand alone to fertile soils which others have already tilled.

❧

Nothing seems quite so old-fashioned as the latest fashion but one.

❧

Raw power is cathartic, but always vulgarizes. Thus, it must never be more than a transition to something more refined.

❧

Indiscriminate tolerance confuses and coarsens our emotions – especially our childish emotions.

❧

We make necessities of our vices at least as often as we make virtues of our necessities.

Moderation is undiscriminating: for it vindicates almost any practice.

❖

Do good and evil, however gauged, not only compete and coexist, but actually cooperate?

❖

All perfection is aggressive.

27

FREEDOM AND ITS TRIALS

Too many options can imprison us more imperceptibly, and thus more securely, than too few.

❖

In an age stripped of moral absolutes, conscience is, more than ever, our last court of appeal.

❖

It is with palpable relief that modernity has discovered 'limits to knowledge'.

❖

It can take far more courage, vision, and discipline to sustain great happiness than to withstand long unhappiness.

❖

Joy, especially when prolonged, can be more unsettling than despair.

❖

The paradox of permissiveness: more individualism, less individuality.

❖

Small decisions seem 'free', large ones fated – and even the proudest will enjoys this sensation of humility.

❖

The interpreter may 'finish' the work of art, but the work of art allows few interpretations to finish *it*.

Everything comes to an end; but nothing is completed.

Long-term prisoners seldom release their
jailers.

❖

Freedom: found only if renounced, mastered
only if negated.

❖

Most values that are open to justification are
vulnerable to repudiation.

❖

Expressive fragments and well-honed effects
may soon be all that stand between the modern
spirit and chaos.

❖

Many can master a moment; few can master a
transition.